Managing Bipolar Disorder

EDITOR-IN-CHIEF

David H. Barlow, PhD

SCIENTIFIC
ADVISORY BOARD

Anne Marie Albano, PhD

Gillian Butler, PhD

David M. Clark, PhD

Edna B. Foa, PhD

Paul J. Frick, PhD

Jack M. Gorman, MD

Kirk Heilbrun, PhD

Robert J. McMahon, PhD

Peter E. Nathan, PhD

Christine Maguth Nezu, PhD

Matthew K. Nock, PhD

Paul Salkovskis, PhD

Bonnie Spring, PhD

Gail Steketee, PhD

John R. Weisz, PhD

G. Terence Wilson, PhD

Managing Bipolar Disorder

A COGNITIVE-BEHAVIORAL APPROACH

Workbook

Michael W. Otto • Noreen A. Reilly-Harrington
Jane N. Kogan • Aude Henin • Robert O. Knauz
Gary S. Sachs

2009

OXFORD
UNIVERSITY PRESS

Oxford University Press, Inc., publishes works that further
Oxford University's objective of excellence
in research, scholarship, and education.

Oxford   New York
Auckland   Cape Town   Dar es Salaam   Hong Kong   Karachi
Kuala Lumpur   Madrid   Melbourne   Mexico City   Nairobi
New Delhi   Shanghai   Taipei   Toronto

With offices in
Argentina   Austria   Brazil   Chile   Czech Republic   France   Greece
Guatemala   Hungary   Italy   Japan   Poland   Portugal   Singapore
South Korea   Switzerland   Thailand   Turkey   Ukraine   Vietnam

Copyright © 2009 by Oxford University Press, Inc.

Published by Oxford University Press, Inc.
198 Madison Avenue, New York, New York 10016

www.oup.com

Oxford is a registered trademark of Oxford University Press

All rights reserved. No part of this publication may be reproduced,
stored in a retrieval system, or transmitted, in any form or by any means,
electronic, mechanical, photocopying, recording, or otherwise,
without the prior permission of Oxford University Press.

ISBN-978-0-19-531337-6 Paper

Printed in the United States of America
on acid-free paper

About Treatments *ThatWork*™

One of the most difficult problems confronting patients with various disorders and diseases is finding the best help available. Everyone is aware of friends or family who have sought treatment from a seemingly reputable practitioner, only to find out later from another doctor that the original diagnosis was wrong or the treatments recommended were inappropriate or perhaps even harmful. Most patients, or family members, address this problem by reading everything they can about their symptoms, seeking out information on the Internet, or aggressively "asking around" to tap knowledge from friends and acquaintances. Governments and healthcare policymakers are also aware that people in need don't always get the best treatments—something they refer to as "variability in healthcare practices."

Now healthcare systems around the world are attempting to correct this variability by introducing "evidence-based practice." This simply means that it is in everyone's interest that patients get the most up-to-date and effective care for a particular problem. Healthcare policymakers have also recognized that it is very useful to give consumers of healthcare as much information as possible, so that they can make intelligent decisions in a collaborative effort to improve physical and mental health. This series, Treatments *That Work*™, is designed to accomplish just that. Only the latest and most effective interventions for particular problems are described in user-friendly language. To be included in this series, each treatment program must pass the highest standards of evidence available, as determined by a scientific advisory board. Thus, when individuals suffering from these problems or their family members seek out an expert clinician who is familiar with these interventions and decides that they are appropriate, they will have confidence that they are receiving the best care available. Of course, only your healthcare professional can decide on the right mix of treatments for you.

This workbook describes a scientifically based and proven effective treatment for managing bipolar disorder. It is designed to be used in conjunction with visits to a qualified mental health professional.

If you suffer from bipolar disorder, this program can be closely integrated with the medication you are taking to help you manage your symptoms and stabilize your mood. Comprised of up to 30 sessions, this treatment is divided into four phases, each with its own focus and set of goals. In phase 1, you will learn the skills and strategies necessary for overcoming the depressive phase of your illness. In phase 2, after your mood has been stabilized, you will work together with your therapist to create a Treatment Contract that informs your friends and family of what to do when you are ill. In phase 3, your therapist will individualize your treatment and focus on specific problem areas such as social skills, problem solving, and anger management. Phase 4 gives advice on the best ways to avoid relapses and shows you how to anticipate future problems. The overall goal of treatment is not to cure your disorder, but to teach you how to manage it effectively so that you can lead a successful and stable life.

David H. Barlow, Editor-in-Chief,
Treatments *ThatWork*™
Boston, MA

Dedications

MWO: For my brother Ken and his family, for your love

NAR-H: For my husband, my parents, and my three precious sons, with all my love

JNK: For my husband Evan, for the love and levity in every day

AH: For the ones who guide and inspire me: my parents, my husband, and my children

ROK: For my son Lucas, who completed the circle of our family

GSS: To James, Leslie, and Gregory, for their endless inspiration and generous patience.

Acknowledgements

This book was designed for clinicians treating individuals with bipolar disorder. It provides a wealth of information and step-by-step clinical strategies for the management of bipolar disorder. These strategies were shaped by our collaborations with a number of teams of clinicians and clinical researchers as well as by the patients with whom we have worked. For their early work, we would like to thank and acknowledge the input from Dina Hirshfeld-Becker and Robert Gould, who initiated a program of group CBT for bipolar disorder at Massachusetts General Hospital. We would also like to thank our collaborators in the Systematic Treatment Enhancement Program for Bipolar Disorder (STEP-BD). Our perspectives on treatment were further influenced by the treatment methods and/or independent studies led by Judith Beck, Aaron T. Beck, Ellen Frank, Dominic Lam, Robert Leahy, David Miklowitz, Cory Newman, Jan Scott, and Ari Zaretsky. Likewise, we learned the value of attending to the promotion of well-being from research by Giovanni Fava. We thank all of these individuals for their valuable input and expanding what is known about the nature and treatment of bipolar disorder.

Contents

Treatment Phase 1 *1*

Chapter 1 Session 1: Introduction *3*

Chapter 2 Session 2: Mood Charting and Activity Scheduling *9*

Chapter 3 Session 3: Cognitive Restructuring—Part I *17*

Chapter 4 Session 4: Cognitive Restructuring—Part II *23*

Chapter 5 Sessions 5 and 6: Cognitive Restructuring—Part III *29*

Chapter 6 Session 7: Core Beliefs *33*

Chapter 7 Session 8: Challenging Core Beliefs *39*

Chapter 8 Session 9: More Work With Core Beliefs *47*

Treatment Phase 2 *53*

Chapter 9 Sessions 10–12: Drafting a Treatment Contract *55*

Chapter 10 Session 13: Hypomanic Cognitive Errors *63*

Treatment Phase 3 *71*

Chapter 11 Problem Solving *73*

Chapter 12 Social Skills *79*

Chapter 13 Breathing and Relaxation *83*

Chapter 14 Anger Management *87*

Treatment Phase 4 *91*

Chapter 15 Improving Well-Being *93*

Chapter 16 The End of Treatment *95*

Appendix of Forms *101*

Treatment Phase 1

Chapter 1 — *Session 1: Introduction*

Goals

- To learn about this program and what it will involve
- To review a model of depression
- To understand the role of your thoughts in your depression
- To discuss the effects of depression on your activity level
- To plan for safety if you are experiencing thoughts of suicide

Overview

You are about to begin a cognitive-behavioral therapy (CBT) program for managing bipolar disorder. This program is comprised of up to 30 sessions with a qualified mental health professional. Treatment is divided into four phases. In the first phase, sessions with your therapist will focus on depression and depressive episodes. In the second phase, you will work with your therapist to devise a Treatment Contract that states what you want to be done in the event that you are experiencing a severe episode (either depressive or manic). It is during this phase that you will choose individuals to be a part of your support system or team. The third phase will target areas such as social skills, anger management, problem solving, anxiety, relaxation, and extreme emotions. In this phase you will learn skills and strategies for decreasing your stress in order to manage depressive and manic symptoms. The final phase of treatment focuses on relapse prevention.

Model of Depression

Depression is more than just the sad mood most people might experience when they have had a bad day. Major depression is a medical disorder that lasts at least 2 weeks and that produces a combination of physical and emotional symptoms that make it very difficult to function in life. Some of these symptoms may include difficulty sleeping, poor concentration, low energy, and loss of appetite, as well as irritability, anger, and increased anxiety and worry.

One of the goals of this program is to teach you about common patterns in depression and how to manage them. You and your therapist will be discussing emotional, cognitive (thought), and behavioral patterns that either serve you well or hurt you and your mood. The goal is to increase the patterns that help and decrease the patterns that hurt through discussion and active practice.

The Role of Cognitions

Cognitions are the thoughts, images, and attitudes that occur on a moment-by-moment basis. Your perceptions and cognitions help define the world for you. These cognitions do not have to be true or accurate to have a powerful effect on your emotions. Oftentimes, faulty cognitions, or what we call "automatic thoughts," can lead to or help maintain depression.

Throughout therapy you will be asked to examine and monitor your mood and automatic thoughts. Right now, because you are depressed, your thoughts are not helping you. You will work with your therapist to identify your negative automatic thoughts and then challenge and alter those negative thoughts to make them more useful for you. This is called cognitive restructuring, and you will learn more about this process later on in treatment.

Depression and Activity Levels

Depression can lead to a decrease in activity level. The feeling of not wanting to do things often keeps people away from positive events in their lives. For example, it is not uncommon for someone who is depressed to say, "I was going to do something, but I ended up just sitting in my room, staring at the wall for an hour and a half." And during that time, it is common for depressed individuals to ruminate (turn negative thoughts over and over in one's head), resulting in an increase in negative thoughts and feelings. In addition, because time was spent staring at the wall instead of getting out and pursuing a positive event, the depressed individual is left with no new experiences and no pleasant memories that would serve as a natural deterrent to depression.

This program of treatment will encourage stepwise reengagement in pleasant and meaningful events. You should think of these events as natural buffers against feelings of depression. However, you do need to be prepared for some of the negative thoughts that will occur when trying to initiate these pleasant events. With depression, it is very common to have self-defeating predictions about events: "I'm not going to have fun anyway. What's the purpose? Why even bother?" Thoughts like these sap the motivation for making the effort to go out. These thoughts also place too much attention on self-evaluation, so that depressed individuals may be plagued by thoughts such as: "Am I having fun yet?" or "Why is it so hard to enjoy anything anymore?" Under these conditions, you can understand that it is a challenge to reengage in pleasant events when depressed. Nonetheless, in this treatment program, you will be asked to do just that. A big part of treatment involves coming up with positive events and participating in them, while monitoring and getting a handle on the negative thoughts that come with depression.

For home practice of therapy principles, you will be asked to monitor your current involvement in work and leisure activities using the Weekly Activity Schedule at the end of the chapter. You will review the completed form with your therapist and begin devising a plan for adding more enjoyable activities and events to your life.

Suicidal Thinking and Self-Care

At times, symptoms of bipolar disorder may include feelings of hopelessness. During intense times when symptoms are at their worst, things may feel so hopeless that life doesn't seem worth living. These feelings might also include thoughts of wanting to harm yourself or commit suicide. Suicidal thoughts can be overwhelming and frightening and may occur during both the depressive and manic phases of the disorder.

The most important thing to remember about suicidal thoughts and behaviors is that they are *symptoms of your illness* and just like other symptoms of bipolar disorder they *can be treated*. If you are experiencing thoughts of suicide, please discuss this with your therapist right away. Your therapist will help you come up with a safety plan and may ask you to review and complete the Self-Care Worksheet for Suicidal Thoughts that appears at the end of this chapter.

Homework

- Complete the Weekly Activity Schedule at the end of the chapter as a first step toward understanding and modifying your usual activities.

- If necessary, review and fill out the Self-Care Worksheet for Suicidal Thoughts.

Weekly Activity Schedule

	Morning	Midday	Afternoon	Evening
Monday				
Tuesday				
Wednesday				
Thursday				
Friday				
Saturday				
Sunday				

Self-Care Worksheet for Suicidal Thoughts

I am aware that suicidal thoughts can be a symptom of depression, and this symptom needs to be managed just like any other symptom of the disorder. These thoughts may come to mind, but it is crucial that I never act on these thoughts; at every point in time, I need to keep myself safe so that I can have a chance to improve. If I do have suicidal thoughts, I have choices other than to act on these thoughts.

My triggers for suicidal thoughts:

_____

_____

_____

_____

_____

I can contact the following people should I ever have strong suicidal thoughts:

My psychiatrist's phone number: _____

My therapist's phone number: _____

My primary support person's phone number: _____

Crisis hotline or emergency room phone number: _____

Other support individuals or resources: _____

Things that I can do to keep myself safe when I am feeling suicidal (places I can go, things I can do, people I can see):

_____

_____

_____

_____

_____

_____

_____

Chapter 2

Session 2: Mood Charting and Activity Scheduling

Goals

- To begin using a Mood Chart to track your symptoms
- To start incorporating pleasant activities into your daily life
- To think about ways of changing your negative thinking by adapting a positive "coaching" attitude

Mood Chart

As part of this program, you will be encouraged to keep a daily record of your mood patterns. Mood charting is recommended because it enables you to detect early signs of changes in your mood and communicate this information to your care providers. Mood charting can also help you and your treatment team to intervene early to prevent severe episodes.

An advantage of mood charting is that you become more familiar with the patterning of your mood and your personal triggers for mood changes. For this reason, there is space on your Mood Chart to note your daily stressors.

You will also be asked to track your medication doses on your Mood Chart. As you know, remembering to take medication can be difficult. Your Mood Chart can help you to keep track of your doses on a daily basis.

You may wish to set up a system of reminders to help you remember to complete your Mood Chart. For example, you can leave reminder notes around your home in places where you are most likely to see them (e.g. bathroom mirror, refrigerator, or inside your front door). You may also wish to set up prompts to help you remember to bring your completed Mood Chart to every session. Your therapist will review your Mood Chart at the beginning of every meeting.

A blank Mood Chart with space to record for an entire month is provided at the end of the chapter.

Completing Your Mood Chart

At first glance the Mood Chart can appear complicated. This is a very common reaction. However, the Mood Chart can take as little as 30 seconds a day to complete. The following directions will help you to fill out your Mood Chart.

At the start of the day:

- Record the number of hours of sleep you got the night before

At the end of the day:

- Rate your mood. Indicate two ratings: one for the highest level your mood reached during the day and one for the lowest level of your mood during the day. If your mood did not change or fluctuate, your two ratings may be the same. If your mood state was normal, you may use the abbreviation WNL, which stands for "within normal limits."

- Rate your anxiety. Use the following scale: No anxiety = 0, Mild anxiety = 1, Moderate anxiety = 2, and Severe anxiety = 3

- Rate your irritability. Use the following scale: No irritability = 0, Mild irritability = 1, Moderate irritability = 2, and Severe irritability = 3

- Make notes on any stressful or positive events that occurred during the day

- Record the number of tablets of each medication actually taken

On a monthly basis:

- Record your weight
- For women, circle the dates when menstruating

Activity Monitoring and Pleasant Events List

For homework last week, you were asked to monitor your current level of activity using the Weekly Activity Schedule. Think about the types of activity you engaged in and the impact they had on your mood.

In this session, you will learn about buffering events. Buffering events are those small activities that a person does week to week that can reliably break up the stress of the week. These activities can be almost anything—watching a favorite television show, taking time to read, working on a hobby, spending time with a friend, scheduling a regular night to go out to dinner—anything that can happen with some regularity. Some people pick a time of the day or a time of the week for such an activity and then change the activity each week, depending on their interests.

In the next few sessions, you will start building in more of these buffering activities. It is helpful to start thinking about some pleasurable events that you may want to add to your life. This is important for treating depression, because depression has a way of sapping motivation and sucking away pleasurable activities in a person's life. The following is a list of pleasant events. Review this list and circle any activities you think you might enjoy, making darker circles around the items you think you might enjoy the most.

Pleasant Events List

    Take daily walks for pleasure
    Jog (at the park, track, or gym)
    Rollerblade
    Ride a bike
    Swim
    Windsurf
    Go sailing
    Fish
    Ski
    Ice skate
    Play a sport (tennis, golf, volleyball, softball, soccer, etc.)
    Train with weights
    Go to a movie
    Have dinner with friends
    Take an art class
    Play with a pet
    Sit in the sun
    Read a book
    Volunteer
    Take up a hobby (drawing, painting, knitting, sewing, etc.)
    Take a cooking or baking class
    Talk to friends on the phone

Write letters
Go window shopping
Learn to play an instrument
Learn a foreign language
Do a crossword puzzle
Barbeque
Go to a spa
Take a bubble bath
Have a garage sale
Plant a garden
Start a collection (stamps, sea glass, sports memorabilia, etc.)
Go to a concert or play
Visit a museum or art gallery
Take a dance class
Plan a vacation
Take a long drive
Rent a DVD and have a movie night with friends
Listen to music
Wash and wax your car
Clean your home
Work on an arts and crafts project
Organize a weekly card game (poker, bridge, cribbage, etc.)
Meditate
Buy flowers for your home
Learn to knit or sew
Play with children

Coaching Story

At the end of this week's session, your therapist will use a metaphor to introduce you to the concept of cognitive restructuring. The purpose of the story is to illustrate how you can accurately evaluate your negative thoughts and how you can change these thoughts by "coaching" yourself with positive self-talk. In short, the coaching story is designed to help you "listen in" and see how you are talking to yourself. The aim is to help you be a useful coach to yourself, making sure that your self-talk helps you with your goals rather than hindering you.

Homework

- Begin mood charting.

- Review the Pleasant Events List and continue to monitor your activities using the Weekly Activity Schedule provided at the end of the chapter.

- Refer back to the coaching story your therapist presented to you and begin to pay attention to the way you coach yourself. Practice replacing "Coach A" thoughts with "Coach B" thoughts instead.

Weekly Activity Schedule

	Morning	Midday	Afternoon	Evening
Monday				
Tuesday				
Wednesday				
Thursday				
Friday				
Saturday				
Sunday				

Mood Chart

Treatments (Enter number of tablets taken each day)							Month/Year Daily Notes	Irritability	Anxiety	Hours Slept Last Night	Depressed — Severe (Significant Impairment NOT ABLE TO WORK)	Depressed — Mod (Significant Impairment ABLE TO WORK)	Depressed — Mild (Without Significant Impairment)	WNL — MOOD NOT DEFINITELY ELEVATED OR DEPRESSED / NO SYMPTOMS / Circle date to indicate Menses	Elevated — Mild (Without Significant Impairment)	Elevated — Mod (Significant Impairment ABLE TO WORK)	Elevated — Severe (Significant Impairment NOT ABLE TO WORK)	Psychotic Symptoms, Strange Ideas, Hallucinations
__ mg	__ mg	Antipsychotic __ mg	Antidepressant __ mg	Anticonvulsant __ mg	Benzodiazepine __ mg	Lithium __ mg / Verbal Therapy												

Rating scale: 0 = none, 1 = mild, 2 = moderate, 3 = severe

MOOD — Rate with 2 marks each day to indicate best and worst

Days: 1–31

Weight

Chapter 3

Session 3: Cognitive Restructuring—Part I

Goals

- To learn to identify common thinking errors
- To begin monitoring your thoughts

Identifying Cognitive Errors

This week, you will learn about common thinking errors and how to increase your awareness and ability to recognize these types of thoughts. As previously mentioned, this process is called cognitive restructuring.

Following is a list of typical thinking styles that can contribute to depression and depressive thoughts. Familiarizing yourself with this list is an important first step in identifying the connections between your thoughts, feelings, and behaviors.

The following are adapted from (Burns, D. 1999. *Feeling Good: The new mood therapy*. New York: Harper Collins.)

All-or-Nothing Thinking (Black-and-White Thinking)

You think in black and white terms; there are no gray areas. This type of thinking is unrealistic because things are seldom all or nothing, good or bad.

Overgeneralization

You assume that a one-time negative occurrence will happen again and again. You use words like "always" or "never" to make generalizations.

Mental Filter

You focus exclusively on negative details and ignore anything positive. Since you are filtering out the positives, you see the entire situation as negative.

Disqualifying the Positive

You turn positives into negatives by insisting they "don't count." This allows you to maintain your negative outlook despite positive experiences.

Jumping to Conclusions

In the absence of solid evidence, you jump to a negative conclusion. There are two types of this: "mind reading" and the "fortune teller error."

Mind Reading

You assume that you know what someone else is thinking. You are so convinced that the person is having a negative reaction to you, you don't even take the time to confirm your guess.

The Fortune Teller Error

You act as a fortune teller who only predicts the worst for you. You then treat your unrealistic prediction as if it were a proven fact.

Magnification (Catastrophizing) or Minimization

You magnify negative things, blowing their importance out of proportion. The outcome of an event appears catastrophic to you.

You minimize positive things, shrinking down their significance. You make good experiences out to be smaller than they are.

Emotional Reasoning

You take your emotions as proof of the way things really are. You assume something is true because you feel it is.

"Should" Statements

You build your expectations with "shoulds," "musts," and "oughts." When you don't follow through, you feel guilty. When others disappoint you, you feel angry and resentful.

Labeling and Mislabeling

You label yourself or someone else, rather than just identifying the behavior.

You mislabel an event by using inaccurate and emotionally extreme language.

Personalization

You take responsibility for things that you don't have control over. You feel guilty because you assume a negative event is your fault.

Self-Monitoring and the Thought Record

As mentioned last week, you will now begin to learn more about cognitive restructuring. Starting today, you will begin to monitor your thoughts using the Thought Record provided at the end of this chapter. This form will help you recognize, evaluate, and modify your automatic negative thoughts, with the goal of improving your mood.

To avoid being needlessly pushed around by inaccurate thoughts, it is important to treat your thoughts as guesses about the world. Before accepting a thought as true, it is important to evaluate the thought to see whether it is truly helpful to you. Whenever you experience a negative thought, you should immediately examine the evidence for and against it. After evaluating the evidence, you should try to come up with an alternative thought that is more realistic. The Thought Record can help you do this.

The Thought Record consists of multiple columns used to separately document the following:

- The event or situation that triggered the automatic thought(s)
- The emotions or feelings associated with the particular event or situation
- The content of the automatic thought(s) and how strongly you believe it
- The accuracy of the automatic thought(s)
- The strength of your emotions and belief in the automatic thought(s) after evaluating the evidence for and against the thought(s)

Figure 3.1 shows an example of a partially completed Thought Record. Your therapist will help you complete your own record in session. For now, you will

Situation	Emotion	Automatic thought	Evaluation of automatic thought	Re-rate emotion
(Describe the event that led to the unpleasant emotion)	(Specify sad, angry, etc., and rate the emotion from 0% to 100%)	(Write the automatic thought and rate your belief in the thought from 0% to 100%)	(Evaluate the accuracy of the automatic thought)	(Re-rate the emotion and your belief in the thought from 0% to 100%)
Fight with my boyfriend	Sad 95%	He doesn't love me anymore. Belief in the thought = 95%		
Thinking about being diagnosed with bipolar disorder	Afraid 90%	Having bipolar disorder means that I'll never reach my life goals. Belief in the thought = 80%		

Figure 3.1
Example of Partially Completed Thought Record

concentrate on monitoring and identifying your thoughts only. You will not begin evaluating and modifying them until next week.

Homework

- Review the list of cognitive errors mentioned in this chapter.
- Use the Thought Record to monitor your thoughts over the course of the next week. For now, you should only fill out the first three columns of the record (situation, emotion, and thought only).
- Continue monitoring your activities and recording them on the Weekly Activity Schedule at the end of this chapter.
- Continue mood charting.

Thought Record

Situation (Describe the event that led to the unpleasant emotion)	Emotion (Specify sad, angry, etc., and rate the emotion from 0% to 100%)	Automatic thought (Write the automatic thought and rate your belief in the thought from 0% to 100%)	Evaluation of automatic thought (Evaluate the accuracy of the automatic thought)	Re-rate emotion (Re-rate the emotion and your belief in the thought from 0% to 100%)

Weekly Activity Schedule

	Morning	Midday	Afternoon	Evening
Monday				
Tuesday				
Wednesday				
Thursday				
Friday				
Saturday				
Sunday				

Chapter 4

Session 4: Cognitive Restructuring—Part II

Goals

- To continue cognitive restructuring by learning to accurately evaluate your thoughts
- To come up with ideas of responsibility-based activities that you can add to your life

Evaluating or Challenging Thoughts

For homework last week, you were instructed to monitor your thoughts using the Thought Record. This week you will learn to evaluate these thoughts. Once you are able to identify thoughts that are related to feelings of depression, then you can question the accuracy of these thoughts. Review with your therapist the thoughts you recorded on the Thought Record and look for common themes. Your goal is to discover how depression distorts your thoughts and to systematically challenge these thoughts so that they no longer have an effect on your mood. For each thought, ask yourself the following:

- "What evidence do I have that this thought is true?"
- "What evidence do I have against this thought?"

Write down your answers to these questions on the Thought Record in the column marked "Evaluation of Automatic Thought." Your therapist will help you practice this step of the process until you feel comfortable doing it on your own. Figure 4.1 shows an example of a fully completed Thought Record with the evaluation column filled out.

Situation (Describe the event that led to the unpleasant emotion)	Emotion (Specify sad, angry, etc., and rate the emotion from 0% to 100%)	Automatic thought (Write the automatic thought and rate your belief in the thought from 0% to 100%)	Evaluation of automatic thought (Evaluate the accuracy of the automatic thought)	Re-rate emotion (Re-rate the emotion and your belief in the thought from 0% to 100%)
Fight with my girlfriend	Sad 95%	She doesn't love me anymore. Belief in the thought = 95%	All couples have arguments. There's a lot of evidence that my girlfriend cares for me and loves me. The argument actually brought up some important issues that we need to work on. If a friend was in this situation, I would tell him not to "overgeneralize."	Sad 25% Belief in the thought = 20%
Thinking about being diagnosed with bipolar disorder	Afraid 90%	Having bipolar disorder means that I'll never reach my life goals. Belief in the thought = 80%	Having bipolar might make it more challenging to reach my goals, but with the right medication and lifestyle changes, I can be successful. I'm engaging in	Afraid 20% Sad 15% Belief in the thought = 20%

Figure 4.1

Example of Completed Thought Record

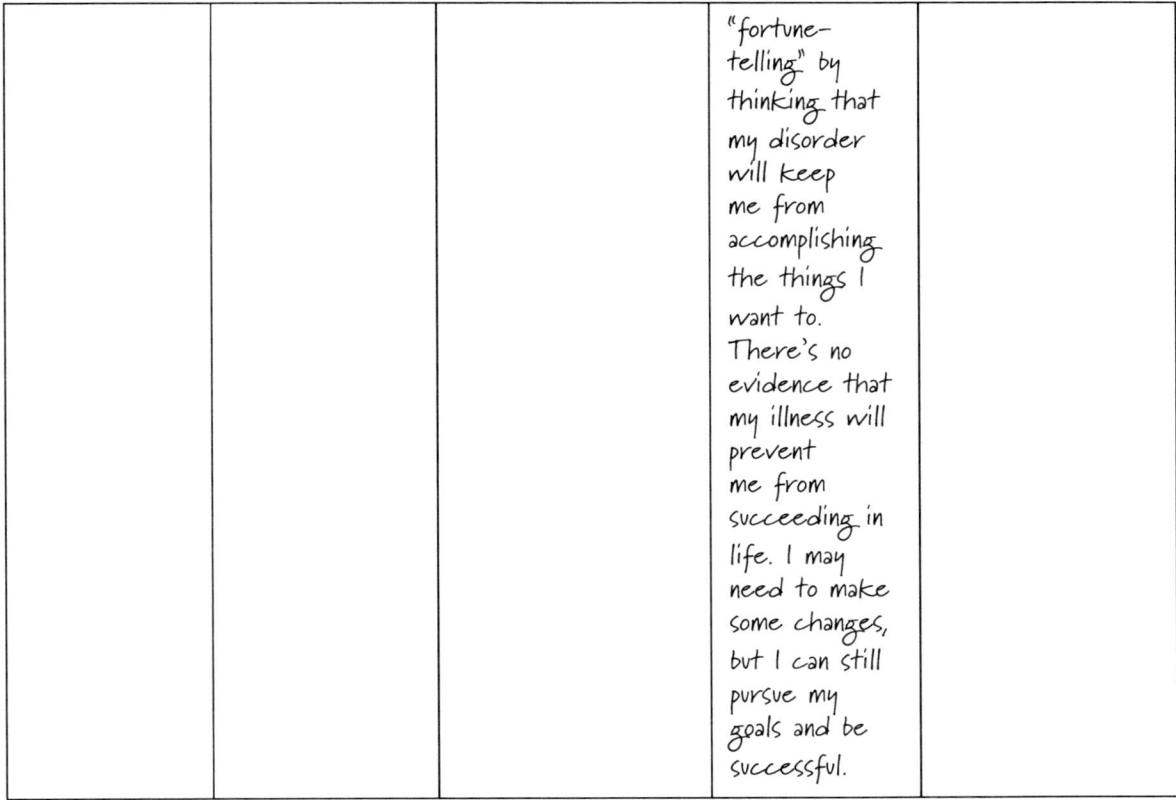

Figure 4.1 *continued*

Activity Planning

The previous session focused on pleasant activities that help buffer stress. This session will focus on adding mastery activities to your schedule. Mastery activities are those that are responsibility based; those things that need to get done, such as doing the laundry, going grocery shopping, and tidying up your home.

Activity scheduling is an important strategy that can be used to enhance your mood. When you are depressed, you may be more likely to stay in bed and less likely to engage in a regular schedule of activities. This restriction of activity is likely to contribute to you feeling even more depressed. The goal of activity scheduling is to devise a plan that allows a gradual reintroduction of regular activity, including both responsibility-based and fun activities.

Work with your therapist to generate ideas for both pleasant and mastery activities that you can add to your life. Record your ideas in the space provided.

My Activities List

Pleasant   Mastery

_____   _____
_____   _____
_____   _____
_____   _____
_____   _____
_____   _____
_____   _____

Homework

- ✏ Continue using the Thought Record to monitor thoughts and feelings on a daily basis. You may now begin completing the evaluation column to challenge negative thinking.

- ✏ Continue adding pleasurable and mastery activities to the My Activities List.

- ✏ Continue monitoring your daily activities using the Weekly Activity Schedule provided at the end of this chapter.

Thought Record

Situation (Describe the event that led to the unpleasant emotion)	Emotion (Specify sad, angry, etc., and rate the emotion from 0% to 100%)	Automatic thought (Write the automatic thought and rate your belief in the thought from 0% to 100%)	Evaluation of automatic thought (Evaluate the accuracy of the automatic thought)	Re-rate emotion (Re-rate the emotion and your belief in the thought from 0% to 100%)

Weekly Activity Schedule

	Morning	Midday	Afternoon	Evening
Monday				
Tuesday				
Wednesday				
Thursday				
Friday				
Saturday				
Sunday				

Chapter 5

Sessions 5 and 6: Cognitive Restructuring—Part III

Goals

- To continue cognitive restructuring by learning to generate more accurate and realistic thoughts

- To make a plan for incorporating both pleasure- and responsibility-based activities into your life

Generating Alternative Responses

Now that you have had practice identifying and evaluating your negative thoughts, it is time to focus on generating alternative thoughts that are more accurate and realistic. For example, if you have the thought, "I am not good at anything I do," and you are able to come up with evidence against this thought, then a reasonable alternative response may be, "There are some things that I don't do well, but there are many things that I'm very good at doing."

Review your previous week's Thought Records with your therapist and come up with some alternative thoughts or interpretations to the negative thoughts you listed.

You are encouraged to continue monitoring your thoughts and completing Thought Records for the next several weeks. The more practice you get now, the easier it will be for you to incorporate a new style of thinking into your daily life. After some additional practice, you can fade out the use of the actual recording form. At that point, you should be comfortable going through the steps of cognitive restructuring in your mind when you sense a change in your mood state.

Planning Activities

Last week you were asked to come up with ideas of pleasurable and mastery activities that you would like to begin incorporating into your life. This week you will begin engaging in these pleasurable activities.

Use the blank Weekly Activity Schedule at the end of this chapter to begin planning your activities for the week. Discuss with your therapist the details of your plan (when, where, and how you will carry out each activity).

The ongoing use of a Weekly Activity Schedule for monitoring and planning daily activities is recommended. Information on the Weekly Activity Schedule (e.g., decreased level of involvement) can serve as an indicator that a more severe depression may be imminent. It can also serve as a device for planning and following through with scheduled events. You are encouraged to complete the Weekly Activity Schedule every evening for the next several weeks.

Homework

- Participate in at least two planned activities this week (one mastery and one pleasurable) and complete the Weekly Activity Schedule at the end of this chapter. Continue to complete the schedule on a nightly basis for the next several weeks. Additional copies of the schedule can be found in the appendix at the end of the book.

- Complete a Thought Record for the week, adding alternative responses and subsequent changes in feeling state. Continue to use the Thought Record over the next several weeks until you are comfortable performing cognitive restructuring on your own. Additional copies of the record can be found in the appendix at the end of the book.

Thought Record

Situation (Describe the event that led to the unpleasant emotion)	Emotion (Specify sad, angry, etc., and rate the emotion from 0% to 100%)	Automatic thought (Write the automatic thought and rate your belief in the thought from 0% to 100%)	Evaluation of automatic thought (Evaluate the accuracy of the automatic thought)	Re-rate emotion (Re-rate the emotion and your belief in the thought from 0% to 100%)

Weekly Activity Schedule

	Morning	Midday	Afternoon	Evening
Monday				
Tuesday				
Wednesday				
Thursday				
Friday				
Saturday				
Sunday				

Chapter 6

Session 7: Core Beliefs

Goals

- To learn about core beliefs and how they relate to your negative thoughts

Introduction to Core Beliefs

Throughout difficult periods in life, people tend to generate beliefs about themselves and how the world works. Many of these beliefs emerge early in life, when we are vulnerable, unsure of ourselves, and just learning about how to navigate life demands and interpersonal relationships. These beliefs also tend to be formed at times of change or crisis, and once formed, these beliefs can become fixed. This means that a belief created when we are young may be applied over and over again across the years, even though the belief is not accurate. These beliefs about ourselves and the world are called *core beliefs*. Core beliefs are often the underlying themes to a range of automatic and dysfunctional thoughts.

Identifying Core Beliefs

There are two strategies to help you with the identification of your core beliefs: top down and bottom up. The bottom-up strategy is to try to infer your core beliefs by examining your responses to early life events. The top-down strategy is to identify themes from your current automatic thoughts. Common themes to automatic thoughts include core beliefs such as "I'm unlovable" or "I am incompetent." These types of negative beliefs may be dormant during times when you are feeling well and activated when you get depressed. When depressed, your core belief may act as a filter. For example, all of the information that supports the negative belief may readily filter through to your daily thoughts, and evidence contradicting the negative belief may be ignored or discounted. These types of negative beliefs can contribute to getting depressed, particularly when negative events happen that relate to your core beliefs. These core beliefs can also be powerful in leading you to avoid or terminate otherwise useful or pleasant situations (e.g., rejecting others before they reject you, leaving a social or work situation).

To start to identify your core beliefs, use the Investigating Underlying Beliefs Worksheet. This form helps you ask questions about automatic thoughts to try to find underlying beliefs. As you write out your automatic thought (use one that is recent, or transfer over a negative automatic thought from one of your recent Thought Records). Then, ask yourself questions about these thoughts to try to identify the beliefs and assumptions about yourself or your performance that may underlie these thoughts. Write in these responses, then investigate further, again asking yourself about assumptions and beliefs that underlie these deeper thoughts. These potential core beliefs should be discussed with your therapist in your next session.

Investigating Underlying Beliefs Worksheet

Automatic thought linked to negative emotion (from Thought Record)

⬇

Investigate the theme behind this thought by answering the following questions: What is the meaning of this thought? Why does this thought bother me? What would be so bad if this thought were true?

⬇

Further investigate underlying beliefs by answering the following questions: What is the meaning of this thought? Why does this thought bother me? What would be so bad if this thought were true?

⬇

What core belief might this reflect?

Homework

- Continue monitoring your automatic thoughts using the Thought Record and examine these thoughts further to determine underlying core beliefs (see appendix for additional copies of Thought Record, if needed).

- If not done in session, complete the Investigating Underlying Beliefs Worksheet.

- Continue monitoring your daily activities using the Weekly Activity Schedule at the end of the chapter (see appendix for additional copies, if needed).

Thought Record

Situation (Describe the event that led to the unpleasant emotion)	Emotion (Specify sad, angry, etc., and rate the emotion from 0% to 100%)	Automatic thought (Write the automatic thought and rate your belief in the thought from 0% to 100%)	Evaluation of automatic thought (Evaluate the accuracy of the automatic thought)	Re-rate emotion (Re-rate the emotion and your belief in the thought from 0% to 100%)

Weekly Activity Schedule

	Morning	**Midday**	**Afternoon**	**Evening**
Monday				
Tuesday				
Wednesday				
Thursday				
Friday				
Saturday				
Sunday				

Chapter 7

Session 8: Challenging Core Beliefs

Goals

- To learn strategies for challenging your core beliefs

Further Understanding Core Beliefs

In the previous session, you used the Investigating Underlying Beliefs Worksheet to begin to identify underlying thoughts that may contribute to your core beliefs. In this session, you will further examine the link between negative and automatic thoughts and the core beliefs they reflect. On the Core Belief Worksheet on page 42, please copy over from your recent Thought Records any recurrent thoughts that you notice. Then, see if you can identify the "theme" behind these thoughts. Also, take some time to think about some of your early memories of times of change or crisis, especially situations where you felt badly. Then try to recall what you came to believe at that time, particularly beliefs about yourself.

The next step is to use this information to try to identify core beliefs that are active during your depression. Write these beliefs and any core strategies (such as avoidance patterns) into the boxes in the middle of the worksheet. Core strategies represent those habits that you used to try to avoid, eliminate, or otherwise cope with core beliefs. Remember that just because you have lots of habits to cope with core beliefs, these habits don't mean your beliefs are true.

Challenging Core Beliefs

When people are depressed, they have a tendency to view their beliefs as facts. Furthermore, they tend to look for support to back up these faulty beliefs. You can challenge core beliefs in much the same way you have been taught to challenge your automatic thoughts. Just as you have been evaluating the evidence for and against your negative thoughts, you will now begin generating evidence contrary to your core beliefs.

Finding Intermediate Beliefs

In restructuring core beliefs, often it is important to find intermediate beliefs that you are willing to accept. For example, if you have the core belief that "I am completely inadequate," it is unlikely that you will go from feeling that way to feeling that you are completely adequate. An intermediate step may be formulating the belief that "I am reasonably adequate at many things." Think about your core beliefs and try to find the middle ground.

Core Beliefs and Childhood Experiences

A crucial part of understanding and modifying core beliefs may involve identifying the developmental and historical precursors of your core beliefs. Choose one of your core beliefs and ask yourself the following questions:

- When did I first feel this way?
- Were there any times in my childhood when I felt this way?

As children, we tend to believe what we are told. In a way, children are like sponges, they absorb what is given to them by their environment. This type of learning can occur in the context of direct messages received from authority figures (parents, teachers, etc.) or from peers. However, sometimes this type of learning occurs more subtly. Sometimes negative messages are given to children unfairly, and they come to believe them as truths. For this reason, it is important for you to explore how you developed certain beliefs about yourself. Then, you can test these beliefs to see if they are fair or realistic now that you are an adult. The following case example illustrates the importance of examining the historical context of core beliefs.

Case Example

Mr. J. had always held the belief that he was inferior and incompetent, particularly in areas related to school and work achievement. The youngest of three brothers, he had relative difficulty in school and was often compared to his older brothers by his parents. He recalls having difficulty in math skills and feeling humiliated by this inadequacy. While he performed relatively well in high school and graduated from a state college, he still felt like a relative failure in contrast to his two older brothers, who graduated from Ivy League schools and pursued law school, like their father. Mr. J. performed well in his job selling life insurance and was well liked by his boss and coworkers. However, when he became depressed, his core beliefs of inadequacy tended to resurface, leaving him doubtful about his abilities and discouraged about his financial situation. Although, he was happily married and owned a home in a pleasant, middle-class neighborhood, he would begin to compare himself to his brothers, who were wealthier and held more prestigious positions in law firms. When depressed, he would also doubt his abilities at work, withdrawing from sales meetings and reducing his client contact. Paradoxically, such behaviors resulted in lower sales figures for the month, further confirming his core beliefs of inadequacy.

An intervention used with Mr. J. involved his view of his own son who was currently in 4th grade (around the same age as Mr. J. was when he developed his core belief of inadequacy). When questioned about how he would treat his son if he had difficulties in school, he began to realize for the first time that he had been treated unfairly. He began to realize that he had skills that his older brothers did not have. However, his parents did not praise those skills and talents (sports, good social skills, etc). Mr. J. began to recognize and evaluate how his core beliefs still pushed him around today. He learned to value some of his talents and to judge himself against his own standards.

Core Belief Worksheet

Situation:	Thought:	Feeling:

Theme behind this thought:

Situation:	Thought:	Feeling:

Theme behind this thought:

Potential Core Belief:
Core Strategies

Age: Situation:
Belief Formed From This Event
Strategy for Dealing With The Event

Age: Situation:
Belief Formed From This Event
Strategy for Dealing With The Event

Age: Situation:
Belief Formed From This Event
Strategy for Dealing With The Event

Source: Form based on strategies in Beck, J. S. (1995). Cognitive theraphy: Basics and beyond. New York: Guilford.

Homework

- Continue using Thought Records to monitor your automatic thoughts and their underlying core beliefs (see appendix for additional copies of the Thought Record, if needed). Remember to generate alternative views to these beliefs.

- If not done in session, complete the Core Beliefs Worksheet.

- Continue scheduling and monitoring activities using the Weekly Activity Schedule at the end of the chapter (see appendix for additional copies, if needed).

Thought Record

Situation (Describe the event that led to the unpleasant emotion)	Emotion (Specify sad, angry, etc., and rate the emotion from 0% to 100%)	Automatic thought (Write the automatic thought and rate your belief in the thought from 0% to 100%)	Evaluation of automatic thought (Evaluate the accuracy of the automatic thought)	Re-rate emotion (Re-rate the emotion and your belief in the thought from 0% to 100%)

Weekly Activity Schedule

	Morning	Midday	Afternoon	Evening
Monday				
Tuesday				
Wednesday				
Thursday				
Friday				
Saturday				
Sunday				

Chapter 8

Session 9: More Work With Core Beliefs

Goals

- To identify the triggers for your depressive episodes
- To refocus on setting and achieving your life goals

Core Beliefs as Triggers for Worsening Mood

In this session, you will begin to explore with your therapist the types of situations that trigger your automatic negative thoughts, and in turn, episodes of depression. You will discuss how these situations may be related to your core beliefs.

The triggers for a depressive episode may differ depending on the nature of your core beliefs. If you place great value on being accepted and loved by others, you may be devastated by losses or rejections, such as the breakup of a romantic relationship or a fight with a close friend or a family member. If you place the greatest value on a need for independence or freedom from control, setbacks at work or criticisms of your abilities may trigger an episode.

Let's return to the case example of Mr. J to illustrate this point.

Case Example

Treatment for Mr. J. was about modifying his core beliefs of inadequacy and helping him target those specific behaviors that served to confirm his core beliefs (e.g., avoiding work responsibilities when depressed). For example, Mr. J. and his therapist targeted specific ways for him to stay on track with clients when feeling depressed. While Mr. J. was usually highly motivated to pursue meetings with clients, he and his therapist acknowledged his tendency to withdraw from clients when depressed. In addition to challenging interfering negative thoughts, he set up a system in which he tracked his number of sales calls per day and discussed this each week during therapy. In this way, he was able to keep his core beliefs from becoming a self-fulfilling prophecy.

My Triggers

Use the space provided to note three typical situations that are likely to trigger negative thoughts related to your core beliefs.

1. _____

2. _____

3. _____

Together with your therapist, you will problem solve alternative cognitive and behavioral responses to these situations.

Readjusting Expectations

This week you will also discuss how your disorder has disrupted your life goals and daily plans. Episodes of mania can be responsible for dramatic disruptions such as missing a semester of school, losing a job, or ending a relationship. Episodes of depression can lead to a loss of motivation, the development of poor work habits, and a disruption in the setting and achieving of goals. During periods of stability, individuals with bipolar disorder may think they need to "catch up" or that they are "falling behind" in their lives. It is important to recognize, however, that trying to make up for lost time only increases anxiety, tension, and stress. This is why you should readjust your personal expectations. Discuss with your therapist the steps you can take toward achieving your goals and complete the Long-Term Goal Sheet.

Long-Term Goal Sheet

Long-term goal:
_____
_____
_____

Short-term goal:

Skill needed to achieve this goal:

Short-term goal:

Skill needed to achieve this goal:

Short-term goal:

Skill needed to achieve this goal:

Short-term goal:

Skill needed to achieve this goal:

Short-term goal:

Skill needed to achieve this goal:

NOW Your current situation: _____
_____
_____

Homework

- Continue to monitor and challenge core beliefs, and explore intermediate beliefs using the Thought Record and, as needed, the Core Belief Worksheet from Chapter 7 (see appendix for additional copies of the Thought Record, if needed).

- Continue scheduling and monitoring activities using the Weekly Activity Schedule at the end of the chapter (see appendix for additional copies, if needed).

Thought Record

Situation (Describe the event that led to the unpleasant emotion)	Emotion (Specify sad, angry, etc., and rate the emotion from 0% to 100%)	Automatic thought (Write the automatic thought and rate your belief in the thought from 0% to 100%)	Evaluation of automatic thought (Evaluate the accuracy of the automatic thought)	Re-rate emotion (Re-rate the emotion and your belief in the thought from 0% to 100%)

Weekly Activity Schedule

	Morning	Midday	Afternoon	Evening
Monday				
Tuesday				
Wednesday				
Thursday				
Friday				
Saturday				
Sunday				

Treatment Phase 2

Chapter 9

Sessions 10–12: Drafting a Treatment Contract

Goals

- To select members of your support system and draft a Treatment Contract

When to Contract

A Treatment Contract is an important element of treatment that can be initiated at any phase, but is typically put into place when individuals are oriented toward relapse prevention. The Treatment Contract makes use of your knowledge about your disorder—the type of symptoms that emerge during the initial stages of mood episodes—to help you put into place protective behaviors. Moreover, by working on the Treatment Contract with both your clinician and your valued family members, you are able to make sure others work with you on your relapse-prevention goals.

Treatment Contract

A Treatment Contract provides you with an opportunity to plan in advance what you want to happen when you are ill. Designing this plan when you are well allows you to specify which management strategies you prefer to use for coping with severe episodes.

Before drafting the contract, you should select individuals to be a part of your support system. You may wish to include your medical doctor(s), your therapist, friends, family members, coworkers, etc. Your support system will participate with you on your Treatment Contract. Use the space provided to list the individuals you'd like to ask to be a part of your support system.

It is important that your support system receive information about bipolar disorder. Advise them to obtain a copy of *Living with Bipolar Disorder: A Guide for Individuals and Families* (Otto et al., 2008, Oxford University Press) and have them read this workbook. You may also invite your support system to attend upcoming meetings with your therapist.

My Support System

_____
_____
_____
_____
_____
_____
_____
_____

Drafting a Treatment Contract

After identifying your support system, you will specify thoughts, feelings, behaviors, and early warning signs for your episodes of depression. Then, you can map out a plan for coping with depression, identifying the ways your support team can help you. You will also note the thoughts, feelings, behaviors, and early warning signs of episodes of hypomania and/or mania. Then, you will map out a plan for coping with these types of episodes, giving specific instructions to your support system. An upcoming session will focus on manic episodes so you may wish to wait until then to devise a plan for dealing with those episodes.

The sample contract at the end of the chapter can be used as a model for developing your own treatment plan.

Homework

- Review and complete the sample Treatment Contract at the end of the chapter. Feel free to personalize the contract and make revisions. Remember, you may wish to hold off on completing the sections related to hypomanic or manic episodes until after you discuss them with your therapist.

- If not done in session, think about who you wish to invite to be a member of your support system.

- If prepared to do so, invite members of your support network to attend upcoming meetings with your therapist.

- Prepare for the upcoming discussion of mania by reflecting on past episodes of mania and the changes in thoughts, feelings, and behaviors that you experienced.

- Continue to complete Thought Records and the Weekly Activity Schedule as advised by your therapist. (See appendix for additional copies of forms.)

Treatment Contract

The purpose of this contract is to organize my care for bipolar disorder, with attention to both the prevention of mood episodes and the efficient treatment of these episodes should they occur. My first step in guiding my care is the selection of my support team. The team members should include people with whom I have regular contact, who can help me identify episodes should they occur and help me put into practice some of the tools discussed in earlier chapters of this workbook.

(Select members of your treatment team to be part of your crew; for example, you may select your psychiatrist, psychologist, social worker, or primary care physician. Other team members may be drawn from the support network identified in Chapter 9.)

Treatment Contract–Support Team		
Role/relationship	Name	Contact information
My Psychiatrist	_____	Phone: _____
My Therapist	_____	Phone: _____
My primary care physician (PCP)	_____	Phone: _____
_____	_____	Phone: _____
_____	_____	Phone: _____
_____	_____	Phone: _____

My second step in developing this contract is to identify tools I will use to help control my bipolar disorder so that I can best pursue my life goals. Many of these tools have been identified in earlier chapters. My goal now is to identify some of the tools that I plan to use

Check Intent to Use

_____ **Monitor my mood for early intervention.**

        Signs of depression and mania are listed in Chapter 1. In addition to these symptoms, I know from my own patterns that I should watch out for the following signs:

        Depressed Thoughts _____

        _____

        Depressed Symptoms _____

        _____

        Depressed Behavior _____

        _____

continued

| | Hypomanic Thoughts | _____ |

| | Hypomanic Symptoms | _____ |

| | Hypomanic Behaviors | _____ |

_____ **Take early action if I notice signs of depression or mania.**

    _____ Contact my psychiatrist at phone # _____.

    _____ Contact my therapist at phone # _____.

    _____ Contact my support person at phone # _____.

    _____ Maintain a regular schedule of sleep and activities.

    _____ Maintain a regular schedule of pleasant events.

    _____ Evaluate my thoughts for negative or hyperpositive thinking.

    _____ Talk with my family about ways to cope.

    _____ Limit my alcohol use and avoid all non-medication drugs.

    _____ Other _____

    _____ Other _____

    _____ Other _____

    _____ Other _____

_____ **Take active steps to keep my mood in the desired range:**

    _____ Take all medications as prescribed by my doctor

    _____ Maintain regular appointments with my psychiatrist of ------/month.

    _____ Maintain regular appointments with my therapist of ------/month.

    _____ Keep a regular sleep schedule.

    _____ Maintain a schedule including at least 3 valued activities each day as a buffer against stress.

    _____ Avoid excessive use of alcohol.

    _____ Avoid all use of illicit drugs.

    _____ Use no alcohol for the next 30 days

    _____ Use no recreational drugs for the next 30 days

continued

Treatment Contract *continued*

- _____ Keep a perspective on my thoughts, and evaluate my thoughts for accuracy
- _____ Share with my family information on communication styles that may reduced stress.
- _____ Other _____
- _____ Other _____
- _____ Other _____
- _____ Other _____

_____ **Contact the following people should I ever have strong suicidal thoughts:**

- _____ Contact my psychiatrist at phone # _____.
- _____ Contact my therapist at phone # _____.
- _____ Contact my support person at phone # _____.
- _____ Other action _____.

_____ **Keep myself safe until I can be seen or go to a local emergency room if I ever fear I may act on suicidal thoughts.**

_____ **If I start to become depressed, I would like my support team to:**

- _____ Talk to me about my symptoms (who _____)
- _____ Make plans for a pleasant event (who _____)
- _____ Discuss ways to reduce stress (who _____)
- _____ Make sure I am taking my medication (who _____)
- _____ Call my doctor if I am unable to (who _____)
- _____ Other _____
- _____ Other _____
- _____ Other _____

_____ **If I start to become manic, I would like my support team to:**

- _____ Talk to me about my symptoms (who _____)
- _____ Talk to me about reducing activities (who _____)
- _____ Allow me to be alone if I am irritable (who _____)
- _____ Take care of the kids/pets/other (who _____)
- _____ Take away my credit cards (who _____)
- _____ Take away my car keys (who _____)

continued

	Take me to the hospital (preferred hospital _____)
	Other _____
	Other _____
	Other _____

I understand that this contract is designed by me so that I can take an active role in my treatment. My goal is to maximize my control by arranging for my treatment team to to take care of me. So that any future decisions are well considered, I agree to change this contract only after giving two weeks written notice to all parties to this contract.

Signatures for contracting individuals

_____ _____
Signature   **Date**   **Signature**   **Date**

_____ _____
Signature   **Date**   **Signature**   **Date**

Chapter 10 Session 13: *Hypomanic Cognitive Errors*

Goals

- To learn to identify errors in thinking that may lead to episodes of mania
- To learn strategies for challenging hyperpositive thinking

Hypomanic Cognitive Errors

In previous sessions, you've talked with your therapist a lot about the warning signs of depression and the types of negative thinking biases that can occur in depression. This week's session will cover the detection and prevention of manic episodes. Think about any of your previous manic or hypomanic episodes. Did you notice that your thinking was hyperpositive during those times?

The following is a list of typical cognitive errors characteristic of hypomania. Review the list and identify any thoughts you have experienced.

- Positive Fortune-Telling—Being overly optimistic about unknown outcomes
- Overreliance on luck—e.g., "I can get away with it."
- Underestimating risk or danger—e.g., "It will work out one way or another."
- Overly positive appraisal of one's talents and abilities—e.g., "I can do no wrong."
- Disqualifying the negative/Minimizing problems/Not thinking through the negative consequences—e.g., "I don't have a care in the world."
- Overvaluing of immediate gratification—e.g., "I want what I want when I want it."
- Suspiciousness or paranoia—e.g., "Everyone is looking at me."
- Misinterpreting the intentions of others—e.g., seeing sexual content or innuendo where there is none ("He/she wants me.") or seeing slights or aggressive content where there is none ("They're out to get me.")

- Inappropriate use of humor—e.g., "They think I'm funny."
- Seeing special connections or heightened religious significance

Challenging Hyperpositive Thinking

The same techniques can be used to examine hyperpositive thinking as are used to challenge your automatic negative thoughts. You may use the Thought Record in the same way. Figure 10.1 shows a completed example of a Thought Record used to examine hyperpositive thinking errors.

Situation	Emotion	Automatic thought	Evaluation of automatic thought	Re-rate emotion
(Describe the event that led to the unpleasant emotion)	(Specify sad, angry, etc., and rate the emotion from 0% to 100%)	(Write the automatic thought and rate your belief in the thought from 0% to 100%)	(Evaluate the accuracy of the automatic thought)	(Re-rate the emotion and your belief in the thought from 0% to 100%)
Received a promotion at work	Elated 90%	I am so much smarter than the CEO and I need to tell her on Monday morning how she should change the company. Belief in the thought = 90%	My therapist has encouraged me to wait before acting impulsively. I may be smarter than my boss and the CEO, but I should probably not tell them what to do. Maybe I can put together a proposal with some of my ideas.	Elated 75% Belief in the thought = 80%—my belief has not decreased that much, but I have a better plan for presenting my ideas at work.

Figure 10.1

Example of Completed Thought Record (responses to hypomanic or irritable thoughts)

			My mood chart reflects that I'm a bit hypomanic right now so maybe I should focus on getting some sleep.	
An attractive man smiled at me on the airplane	Excited 90%	He wants me. I should go talk to him. Belief in the thought = 90%	He might think I'm attractive, but it doesn't necessarily mean that he wants me. These types of thoughts have gotten me into trouble in the past. Besides, I'm married and want to stay faithful to my husband. I'm a bit elevated and feeling hypersexual right now.	Excited 70% Belief in the thought = 50%

Figure 10.1 *continued*

Minimizing the Impact of Hypomania and Mania

Now that you understand how to identify and examine your hyperpositive thoughts, you can begin implementing strategies for preventing episodes of mania that may follow these thoughts. A primary strategy is talking with your therapist and your psychopharmacologist to consider whether a medication change may be helpful in ensuring that hypomanic symptoms do not escalate into full mania.

Another important strategy is in considering how you can ensure that temporary hypomanic or manic symptoms do not lead to longstanding regret. With hypomania and mania a wide range of risky behaviors—financial decisions, investments, romantic liaisons, sexual behavior, substance use, or interpersonal confrontations—may *feel* appropriate due to the expansive mood of mania. Part of managing hypomania is to avoid making impulsive decisions and to avoid trusting the overpositive mood and thinking that is at the core of hypomania and mania. Even though a decision may *feel right*, it may not *be right* in mania. This is crucial to remember, because arguments with family members or employers, financial blunders, sexual affairs, or substance abuse all have consequences that greatly outlast the hypomanic or manic episode. To help combat this potential for negative outcomes, it is helpful to follow the following principles for action when hypomanic symptoms are present. Some of these principles are already included in the Treatment Contract, but you may want to include additional rules to help protect yourself from negative consequences from hypomania and mania.

During hypomanic or manic episodes, it is important to:

- Avoid major financial decisions such as new purchases or major investments. This is done to protect your financial security, so that your long-term financial health is not challenged by the consequences of *overconfidence* from mania. If you feel like you must make a decision when you are feeling positive or high, it is best to check with at least two valued advisors to help you decide whether the decision is sound. This is called the Two-Person Feedback Rule. Because a hypomanic mood may lead you to believe that you are thinking faster and better than those around you, it is crucial that you do not discount the advice from these valued advisors.

- Avoid alcohol and drug use when hypomanic. When hypomanic, you may feel like you can handle alcohol or drug use; it is crucial at these times to know that your judgment is impaired by the mood episode. No good can come from mixing alcohol and drug use with hypomania.

- Avoid relationship decisions. When hypomanic, don't give out your phone number, ask out new people, or engage in sexual behavior with new partners.

- Avoid confrontations. Hypomania and mania often bring irritability. When irritability is high, it may well be worth protecting your job or your relationships by taking a day off work or agreeing with you family members to not have major discussions ("I am really irritable these days from my mood, let's put off any major discussions until I feel better. And if I seem especially caught up on minor issues, know that these issues may be much more manageable for me when my mood normalizes.").

- Avoid using a credit card when hypomanic. When mood episodes strike, you may want to turn over any credit cards with high spending limits to a valued other so that you cannot create substantial debt for yourself during the episode.

Homework

- If not completed, finalize your Treatment Contract, with attention to the type of thinking and activity patterns that characterize the emergence of hypomanic or manic episodes.

- Use the Thought Record to monitor your hyperpositive thinking, as well as your negative automatic thoughts.

- Continue scheduling and monitoring activities using the Weekly Activity Schedule (see appendix for additional copies of the form).

Thought Record

Situation (Describe the event that led to the unpleasant emotion)	Emotion (Specify sad, angry, etc., and rate the emotion from 0% to 100%)	Automatic thought (Write the automatic thought and rate your belief in the thought from 0% to 100%)	Evaluation of automatic thought (Evaluate the accuracy of the automatic thought)	Re-rate emotion (Re-rate the emotion and your belief in the thought from 0% to 100%)

Weekly Activity Schedule

	Morning	Midday	Afternoon	Evening
Monday				
Tuesday				
Wednesday				
Thursday				
Friday				
Saturday				
Sunday				

Treatment Phase 3

Chapter 11 *Problem Solving*

Overview of Phase 3 of Treatment

In this phase of treatment, your therapist will work with you to target specific issues or problems you are having. From now on, session content will be individualized and tailored to fit your specific needs. The next four chapters represent some of the topics your therapist may address with you during this stage of treatment.

Introduction to Problem Solving

The first topic is problem solving. You may have noticed that when you are depressed you have a hard time resolving certain issues or problems. This is because depression makes it hard to view situations accurately and realistically. Problem solving teaches you how to evaluate and solve problems more efficiently by considering numerous alternative solutions. Problem solving considers all solutions as viable until they are evaluated more closely.

Scheduling a Time for Solving Problems

To help keep worry out of your life, establish one or two specific times in your weekly schedule for dealing with life issues. By focusing on life issues as a regular part of the week, you will help ensure that life's problems do not become overwhelming. Try to devote at least one hour every week to evaluating your life issues using the Problem-Solving Worksheet and the method described in the following section. Make note of your problem-solving schedule in the space provided.

My Problem-Solving Schedule
My regular problem-solving times will be:
_____ (time) on _____ (day of the week) and / or
_____ (time) on _____ (day of the week)

Steps to Problem Solving

Components of a traditional problem solving approach include the following:

1. Identifying the problem
2. Clearly defining the problem (what about the situation makes it bothersome?)
3. Brainstorming a list of all possible solutions, even those that may seem silly or impossible
4. Evaluating the solutions (advantages and disadvantages of each)
5. Selecting a solution or combination of solutions (taking into account the benefits and liabilities of each solution)
6. Implementing the solution
7. Evaluating the effectiveness of the solution

This method does not guarantee that you will come up with a good solution, but it will ensure that you think about problems more effectively and take the time to examine the best solutions you can think of on any given day. To guide you in this process, review the sample, completed Problem-Solving Worksheet shown in Figure 11.1. A blank copy of the sheet for your own use is also provided. Use the worksheet at your scheduled problem-solving times to evaluate difficult life situations and generate possible solutions. Additional copies of the sheet can be found in the appendix at the end of the book.

Problem-Solving Worksheet

What is the problem:

Arguments with my spouse about money

Why does this problem bother me (what are the specific features that bother me)?

I want a better sense of control over our finances.

I feel like I'm the only one who really cares what happens with our money.

Is this a realistic problem (e.g., what do I really think is going to happen, and what part of this problem do I think is just worry)?

Yes, we really argue quite often about money

How can I rewrite the problem clearly, so that it helps me think about a solution? Write in a clear restatement of the problem:

My spouse and I don't plan how to spend money, and then we're surprised by what each of us has spent. This always leads to an argument.

Now that I have the problem clearly in mind, what are potential solutions to this problem? To generate solutions, I want to think about as many possible solutions as possible (without thinking why they are good or bad, and without choosing an option at this point). What advice might a good friend give? If a friend had this problem, what advice would I give?

Potential options:

1. Just keep doing what we're doing.
2. Set up a weekly meeting where my spouse and I can discuss our finances and the household budget.
3. Open separate bank accounts.
4. Use a notebook to track expenses and review with one another on a weekly basis.
5. Assign a small amount of money as "free use" money and create a stricter budget for managing the rest.

Now rate each potential option. For each option rate the good and bad aspects of the proposed solution. Do not select an option until each is rated.

Figure 11.1

Example of Completed Problem-Solving Worksheet

Good things about each solution	Bad things about each solution
1. No effort required	Nothing is resolved and things may get worse
2. Gives us a chance to talk openly about money	We may end up fighting during meetings
3. Gives each of us a sense of freedom	I would feel like we aren't partners
4. Makes each of us accountable and makes sure we talk to each other about money	May be hard to remember to use the notebook
5. Like option #3, this gives us more freedom	We really should be buying things together, as a couple

Given this evaluation, which solution seems best?

Options 2 and 4 seem like the best solutions. Tracking our finances and meeting weekly seems to be a good way to start changing the situation.

Do you want to apply this solution, or is more time or more information needed to solve this problem?

Yes, I think we can start having meetings and using a notebook to track our finances. I really want to change things and avoid arguments over money.

Figure 11.1 *continued*

Problem-Solving Worksheet

What is the problem:
_____

Why does this problem bother me (what are the specific features that bother me)?
_____
_____
_____

Is this a realistic problem (e.g., what do I really think is going to happen, and what part of this problem do I think is just worry)?
_____

How can I rewrite the problem clearly, so that it helps me think about a solution? Write in a clear restatement of the problem:
_____
_____

Now that I have the problem clearly in mind, what are potential solutions to this problem? To generate solutions, I want to think about as many possible solutions as possible (without thinking why they are good or bad, and without choosing an option at this point). What advice might a good friend give? If a friend had this problem, what advice would I give?

Potential options:
_____
_____
_____
_____
_____
_____

Now rate each potential option. For each option rate the good and bad aspects of the proposed solution. Do not select an option until each is rated.

Good things about each solution   Bad things about each solution

1.
2.
3.
4.
5.
6.

Given this evaluation, which solution seems best?
_____

Do you want to apply this solution, or is more time or more information needed to solve this problem?
_____

Chapter 12 *Social Skills*

Introduction to Social Skills

Many individuals with bipolar disorder experience difficulties with social situations. The goal of this part of treatment is to help you improve your social skills. For some people, this will be a chance to hone skills with which they never felt fully comfortable. For other individuals, this will be an opportunity to learn to undo limitations in social skills that may have grown out of periods of depression. There are two kinds of skills your therapist may work with you on. The first are general social skills, which include things like smiling, laughing, and making eye contact. General social skills refer to both verbal and nonverbal methods of communicating. The second skill you will work on is assertiveness.

Hierarchy of Social Situations

The first step in improving your social skills is to work with your therapist to create a hierarchy of social situations that may be hard for you. Examples include saying hello to a stranger, starting a conversation with a coworker, or going to a party alone. Think about the social situations that you have experienced in the past and use these to help you create your hierarchy. Use the form provided, and list the situations in order of difficulty. Use a scale of 0–100 to rate each item, where 0 represents no difficulty and 100 represents the most difficulty.

Your therapist will engage you in role-play exercises where you imagine yourself in one of the scenarios from your hierarchy. Eventually, you will be asked to participate in some of these situations in real life so you can practice what you have learned in treatment.

Hierarchy of Social Situations

Situation	Level of Difficulty (0–100)

General Social Skills Training

One of the most valuable social skills you can learn is effective listening. Effective listening refers to the skill of making sure that you accurately hear the speaker's message and accurately communicate to the speaker that you heard it. To be an effective listener it is important to try to understand what the speaker is actually saying. The following steps are essential to effective listening:

- Give the speaker clear signs that you are listening to what he or she is saying. Look the speaker in the eye and nod as you hear each point.

- Ask questions to clarify individual points. Your goal is to understand the speaker's perspective.

- Verify that you have heard the speaker's issues correctly by repeating the core content to the speaker.

- Once you and the speaker agree on the message, then it is your turn to respond.

Assertiveness Training

Before you can learn to be assertive, you need to understand the difference between assertive, aggressive, and passive behaviors. Nonassertive behaviors increase stress levels and feelings of frustration. Being passive can cause a build-up of resentment, which can negatively impact your relationships. Being aggressive may increase conflict with others, as well as feelings of shame, guilt, or regret.

Passivity can be defined as a way of behaving whereby we pay a great deal of attention to others' needs, rights, and wishes, but minimize or ignore our own. Aggressiveness refers to a pattern of behavior where we demand that our own wishes, needs, and rights be considered while paying little attention to the needs of others. In contrast, assertiveness is a way of behaving that respects everyone's wishes, needs, and rights.

Review the following scenarios and work with your therapist to come up with passive, aggressive, and assertive responses to each one.

- Someone asks you for a ride home and it is inconvenient for you because you have several errands to run and the drive will take you out of your way. What can you say?
- You would like to ask your boss for a raise. What do you say?
- A pushy salesperson is trying to convince you to buy a stereo that is significantly more expensive than what you had planned to spend. How do you respond?
- You've been waiting for 20 min in line at the bank. Suddenly, someone cuts in front of you. What do you say?
- The phone rings as you are preparing dinner—it's a good friend of yours. How can you handle the situation?
- Your friend asks to borrow money for the second time this month—you have some extra money that you've been putting aside to buy something that you've wanted for a long time. What do you tell him?

Effective assertiveness communication requires two basic skills. First, you must be able to take a step back from the situation and reflect on the course of action to be taken. Second, you must respond to situational demands in an assertive manner. The first step can be broken down into the following series of behaviors:

- Decreasing emotional arousal—taking a step back from the situation to calm down; going for a walk; doing a brief relaxation exercise such as deep breathing.

- Clarifying the nature of the problem. Examining your own feelings and thoughts about the situation.

- Identifying any distorted patterns of thinking that may be impacting your ability to behave effectively in the situation. Challenging negative, unrealistic, or judgmental thinking patterns.

- Deciding on which behavior(s) may be appropriate. For example, letting go of the situation versus expressing your feelings to the other person involved.

The second step of assertiveness training focuses on communication skills. Assertive communication entails:

- Describing the situation to the other person. Reporting the facts as objectively as possible, attempting not to mix in feelings. The reporting should be situation-specific and refer to the current problem at-hand, rather than bringing up a series of past difficulties.

- Expressing feelings about the situation using "I" statements, as opposed to "You." For example, saying, "I feel upset when . . . " versus, "You messed up when . . . " By taking responsibility for your feelings, you are more likely to get a positive, nondefensive reaction from others.

- Asking for what you want in a straightforward, specific manner.

- Explaining how the suggested change will be beneficial to everyone involved. Making a positive statement about the other person.

Chapter 13 *Breathing and Relaxation*

Introduction to Breathing and Relaxation Skills

Breathing and relaxation skills are helpful methods for managing anxiety and stress. Once learned, these skills can be useful if applied whenever you feel anxious, angry, irritable, or frustrated.

Diaphragmatic Breathing

To learn how to breathe in a calming manner, sit with one hand on your chest and the other hand on your abdomen, just above your navel. As you breathe, notice the rise and fall of your hands. During proper diaphragmatic breathing, your abdomen (not your chest) should expand as you breathe in and contract as you breathe out. Perfecting this technique takes practice, so we have provided the following instructions to guide you.

Step 1: Rest comfortably in a chair

Step 2: Place one hand on your chest and the other just below your rib cage

Step 3: Breathe in slowly through your nose so that your stomach expands outward. The hand on your chest should remain still.

Step 4: Breathe out through your mouth so that your stomach contracts. The hand on your chest should remain still.

You may find that it is easier to practice this method while lying down. As you gain more practice, you can try the technique while sitting in a chair. During your first few exercises, you may feel mildly lightheaded. To combat this feeling, you may want to time your breaths. For example, you can count from 1 to 3 as you breathe in and then count from 1 to 5 as you breathe out. Alternatively, you can use the word "relax" to time your breathing. You can softly say to yourself the word "relax" as your breathe ("Reee" on the inhale and "laaaax" on the exhale).

Practice makes perfect, so be sure to engage in breathing exercises at least twice a day for 5 min at a time.

Progressive Muscle Relaxation

Progressive muscle relaxation (PMR) is a useful skill for reducing tension and stress and promoting a sense of well-being. PMR is about utilizing repeated tension (10 seconds) and relaxation (20 seconds) procedures for a selected set of muscle groups. Following are instructions for practicing an 8-muscle PMR exercise.

8-Muscle PMR

1) Arms Muscle Group

Slowly draw both hands into fists. Pull your fists into your chest and hold for 10 seconds, squeezing as tight as you can. Then, slowly release while you count for 20 seconds. Notice the feeling of relaxation.

2) Legs Muscle Group

Slowly increase the tension in your quadriceps and calves over 10 seconds by lifting your legs slightly off the floor and pointing your feet inward. Squeeze the muscles as hard as you can. Then, gently lower your legs and relax your feet, releasing the tension over 20 seconds. Notice the tension melting away and the feeling of relaxation that is left.

3) Stomach Muscle Group

Make your stomach hard by pulling your stomach in toward your spine very tightly. Feel the tightness of your stomach muscles. Focus on that part of your body, and hold the tension for 10 seconds. Then, let your stomach relax outwards over 20 seconds.

4) Chest Muscle Group

Take a deep breath and hold it for 10 seconds. Then, let the air escape and breathe normally for 20 seconds, letting the air flow in and out smoothly and easily. Feel the difference as the muscles relax.

5) Shoulders and Upper Back Muscle Group

Pull your shoulder blades back and together. Feel the tension around your shoulders and radiating down into your back. Hold for 10 seconds. Relax your shoulder blades over 20 seconds and let them return to a normal position. Focus on the sense of relaxation around your shoulders and across your upper back.

6) Neck Muscle Group

Build up the tension around your neck by pulling your chin down toward your chest and raising and tightening your shoulders. Focus on the tension and hold for 10 seconds. Then, release the tension over 20 seconds, letting your head rest comfortably and your shoulders droop. Concentrate on the relaxation.

7) Mouth, Jaw, and Throat Muscle Group

Tense the muscles around your mouth, jaw, and throat by clenching your teeth and forcing the corners of your mouth into a forced smile. Hold for 10 seconds. Then, release the tension over 20 seconds, letting your mouth drop open and the muscles around your throat and jaw relax. Concentrate on the difference in the sensations in that part of your body.

8) Eyes and Forehead Muscle Group

Squeeze your eyes tightly shut while pulling your eyebrows down and toward the center. Feel the tension across your lower forehead and around the eyes. Concentrate on the tension and hold for 10 seconds. Then, release the tension over 20 seconds. Relax the forehead, smoothing out the wrinkles.

Chapter 14   *Anger Management*

Introduction to Anger Management

Anger and irritability are relatively common elements of both depressed and (hypo)manic mood states. The goal of this part of treatment is to help you manage anger and confrontational behaviors more effectively. To achieve this goal, your therapist will teach you several skills for handling the emergence as well as the escalation of anger. The following principles are designed to help you reduce irritability and episodes of anger.

1. Don't let poor thinking habits goad you into an angry outburst or argument.

2. Just because you are irritated, does not mean you have to solve the issue right away.

3. Beware of win or lose thinking (thinking that you have to *act now* to avoid losing).

4. Remember to value your life goals, even when you're angry.

The sections that follow provide information on putting these principles to use.

Poor Thinking Habits and Anger

When you are feeling irritated, it is important to be able to quickly evaluate and defuse the thoughts you are having that can turn small annoyances into full-blown anger episodes. There are two types of anger-related thoughts to watch out for. The first type of thought serves to bring past annoyances and frustrations into the present, so that any minor annoyance becomes associated with these old emotions. Following is a list of some common magnifying thoughts.

- This is just like last time.

- He is always doing this to me.

- Here we go again; this is endless.

- I am always being treated this way.
- I can't let this happen again.

The second type of magnifying thought is one where you are guessing at the motives of others. The following thoughts have the effect of increasing a sense of victimization and anger.

- He is doing this on purpose, to mess with me.
- He thinks my feelings are unimportant.
- He has no respect for me.
- I am sick and tired of being manipulated.
- They are out to get me.

It is important to recognize these thoughts as you have them, so you can successfully coach yourself through conflicts. The idea is to reduce the impact of your anger and irritability on your relationships and personal goals.

Solving the Issue Right Away

Anger can cloud your perception of a particular issue or event. If you are angry or frustrated, you may feel that you need to solve the issue at hand *right away*. However, it is always a better idea to give yourself some time to cool down before making a rash decision in an effort to solve the problem that very minute.

Win or Lose Thinking

Thinking about having to win an argument can prevent you from making more useful choices in a time of irritability and anger. Even when you know that stopping an argument is the best option, your anger and frustration may keep you in the mood to prolong the conflict. Try to avoid this at all costs. Remind yourself that you don't need to win the argument. Instead, you need to maximize how well your life is going.

Value Your Life Goals

Don't let your anger get in the way of pursuing and achieving your life goals. When you feel irritated or frustrated, ask yourself what you can do at that moment that would *serve you* better than getting angry. Guide yourself toward effective and calm action.

Behavioral Analysis

The first step in anger management is to think about a time when you became angry, irritable, or frustrated and conduct a step-by-step analysis of the event. It is important to identify as many thoughts, behaviors, and feelings that preceded the angry outburst as possible. Your therapist will work with you to conduct the analysis and show you how you can use cognitive restructuring and problem-solving techniques to avoid anger episodes in the future. As a first step, you should begin using the Thought Record to identify the thoughts that tend to increase your anger. These are your warning signs. Once you become familiar with your warning signs and how to recognize them early on, you can then begin to manage them, giving you more power over your angry reactions. Use the Thought Record over the next several weeks. Additional copies can be found in the appendix at the end of the book.

Thought Record

Situation (Describe the event that led to the unpleasant emotion)	Emotion (Specify sad, angry, etc., and rate the emotion from 0% to 100%)	Automatic thought (Write the automatic thought and rate your belief in the thought from 0% to 100%)	Evaluation of automatic thought (Evaluate the accuracy of the automatic thought)	Re-rate emotion (Re-rate the emotion and your belief in the thought from 0% to 100%)

Treatment Phase 4

Chapter 15 — *Improving Well-Being*

Introduction to Well-Being Therapy

Over the last few months in treatment, you have learned a wide range of strategies for better managing your disorder. Most of these strategies were directed at reducing mood episodes and those situations and events that can trigger them. To complement the work you've done so far, this phase of the program will focus on increasing your positive emotions and feelings of well-being.

Well-being refers to moments when you feel happy and satisfied. This is not to be confused with periods of hypomania, however. We are not referring to moments of particular excitement, achievement, or superiority, but of much quieter moments of well-being.

As a first step toward focusing on increasing pleasure and maximizing your enjoyment of life, it is important to clearly define your "meaning of life." What is the purpose of life for you? What is it all about? What are you supposed to do while you are alive, and what is the role of fun, of work, and of relationships in your life? Use the space provided to define those things that are important to you in life.

My Meaning of Life

_____

_____

_____

_____

_____

_____

Now that you have clearly identified and defined the areas of life that are most important to you, the next step is to begin monitoring your periods of well-being.

Buy a journal or notebook that appeals to you and represents who you are and use it as your well-being diary. The purpose of a well-being diary is to help you recognize and attend to the pleasant moments in life. Use the diary nightly to record the times that day when you felt most happy and satisfied. Write down the day, time, and the situation, as well as the thoughts and feelings you had at the time you were feeling well. Over time, the well-being diary becomes a catalog of the times in your life that are working well. Use this catalog to review and plan for more periods of well-being in your life. Be sure to bring your diary with you to the remaining sessions. Your therapist will review your diary and help you come up with ways of continuing periods of well-being.

In addition to recording the pleasant moments in your life, we want to make sure that you are adept at "echoing" and increasing these moments. Echoing refers to the process of making sure that a pleasant event has reverberations during the day. If you take a moment each day to reflect on a period of well-being, you are more likely to plan additional pleasant activities and reduce the likelihood that you will experience a depressed mood. The goal is for you to become good at noticing the range of situations and events that increase your well-being and use this information to enhance those feelings in your life.

Chapter 16   *The End of Treatment*

As you have discussed with your therapist, the end of a formal treatment program should not be the end of your treatment. Instead, the end of regular sessions with your therapist signals the beginning of your own program of therapy to extend your treatment gains. That is, cognitive-behavioral therapy (CBT) is not just a method of short-term treatment; it is an ongoing way of approaching life issues. After formal treatment ends, we want you to continue to apply the same caring, problem-solving focus that you used in formal treatment.

Treatment emphasized the role of thoughts, activities, and problem solving in enjoying life. You learned not to accept automatic thoughts but to monitor and evaluate the ideas going through your mind. In addition, you were introduced to the idea of using thoughts in self-coaching, to make sure that you are actively guiding yourself effectively in life. You also devoted time to assessing your schedule and making sure that your schedule supported you and your interests, including break times and pleasant events as well as times for working on your goals. All of these strategies were introduced in the context of a step-by-step review of life problems and potential solutions. We want you to keep this focus on solutions and increasing periods of well-being.

To help you complete your transition to managing your own treatment, we have provided you with Review Sheets. These sheets are designed to remind you to take an active part in your treatment and to underscore the importance of occasional reviews of progress and problems. We want you to treat each review as if it were a return visit to therapy. In fact, take a moment right now to schedule appointments with yourself. On the following pages, write in the appointment dates for sessions, and then hold the sessions with yourself at the appointed times. These brief reviews of symptoms and methods should help you maintain and extend your treatment gains.

Maintaining treatment gains does not mean that you always will be in a good mood in the future. In fact, we guarantee that you will have some difficulties with your mood sometime in the next several months. We guarantee it because almost everyone has these difficulties as a result of stress or other life issues. When this happens, take the experience as a signal that you need to review the skills you learned in treatment and put them to use. If you experience symptoms of mania, then you already know to contact your physician as soon as possible to evaluate your medication needs. Likewise, if stronger feelings of sad or blue mood persist, make sure to contact your doctor and keep applying the skills you learned in treatment.

At any point, you may want to contact your therapist for a "tune-up." Sometimes a brief meeting with a therapist can go a long way in helping you continue on the right track with your goals.

1-Month Review Sheet

Date of Review _____

1. What skills have you been practicing well, and how are you coaching yourself?

   _____
   _____
   _____

2. Where do you still have troubles, and what concerns do you have about these troubles?

   _____
   _____
   _____

3. What skills do you need to practice?

   _____
   _____
   _____

4. List your treatment goals for the next several months.

   _____
   _____
   _____

5. What positive events are you going to plan so that you have pleasant memories to look back on? Remember that even small events can go a long way toward increasing happiness.

   _____
   _____
   _____

3-Month Review Sheet

Date of Review _____

1. What skills have you been practicing well, and how are you coaching yourself?

   _____
   _____
   _____

2. Where do you still have troubles, and what concerns do you have about these troubles?

   _____
   _____
   _____

3. What skills do you need to practice?

   _____
   _____
   _____

4. List your treatment goals for the next several months.

   _____
   _____
   _____

5. What positive events are you going to plan so that you have pleasant memories to look back on? Remember that even small events can go a long way toward increasing happiness.

   _____
   _____
   _____

6-Month Review Sheet

Date of Review _____

1. What skills have you been practicing well, and how are you coaching yourself?

   _____
   _____
   _____

2. Where do you still have troubles, and what concerns do you have about these troubles?

   _____
   _____
   _____

3. What skills do you need to practice?

   _____
   _____
   _____

4. List your treatment goals for the next several months.

   _____
   _____
   _____

5. What positive events are you going to plan so that you have pleasant memories to look back on? Remember that even small events can go a long way toward increasing happiness.

   _____
   _____
   _____

Appendix of Forms

Thought Record

Situation (Describe the event that led to the unpleasant emotion)	Emotion (Specify sad, angry, etc., and rate the emotion from 0% to 100%)	Automatic thought (Write the automatic thought and rate your belief in the thought from 0% to 100%)	Evaluation of automatic thought (Evaluate the accuracy of the automatic thought)	Re-rate emotion (Re-rate the emotion and your belief in the thought from 0% to 100%)

Thought Record

Situation (Describe the event that led to the unpleasant emotion)	Emotion (Specify sad, angry, etc., and rate the emotion from 0% to 100%)	Automatic thought (Write the automatic thought and rate your belief in the thought from 0% to 100%)	Evaluation of automatic thought (Evaluate the accuracy of the automatic thought)	Re-rate emotion (Re-rate the emotion and your belief in the thought from 0% to 100%)

Thought Record

Situation (Describe the event that led to the unpleasant emotion)	Emotion (Specify sad, angry, etc., and rate the emotion from 0% to 100%)	Automatic thought (Write the automatic thought and rate your belief in the thought from 0% to 100%)	Evaluation of automatic thought (Evaluate the accuracy of the automatic thought)	Re-rate emotion (Re-rate the emotion and your belief in the thought from 0% to 100%)

Thought Record

Situation (Describe the event that led to the unpleasant emotion)	Emotion (Specify sad, angry, etc., and rate the emotion from 0% to 100%)	Automatic thought (Write the automatic thought and rate your belief in the thought from 0% to 100%)	Evaluation of automatic thought (Evaluate the accuracy of the automatic thought)	Re-rate emotion (Re-rate the emotion and your belief in the thought from 0% to 100%)

Thought Record

Situation (Describe the event that led to the unpleasant emotion)	Emotion (Specify sad, angry, etc., and rate the emotion from 0% to 100%)	Automatic thought (Write the automatic thought and rate your belief in the thought from 0% to 100%)	Evaluation of automatic thought (Evaluate the accuracy of the automatic thought)	Re-rate emotion (Re-rate the emotion and your belief in the thought from 0% to 100%)

Weekly Activity Schedule

	Morning	Midday	Afternoon	Evening
Monday				
Tuesday				
Wednesday				
Thursday				
Friday				
Saturday				
Sunday				

Weekly Activity Schedule

	Morning	Midday	Afternoon	Evening
Monday				
Tuesday				
Wednesday				
Thursday				
Friday				
Saturday				
Sunday				

Weekly Activity Schedule

	Morning	Midday	Afternoon	Evening
Monday				
Tuesday				
Wednesday				
Thursday				
Friday				
Saturday				
Sunday				

Weekly Activity Schedule

	Morning	Midday	Afternoon	Evening
Monday				
Tuesday				
Wednesday				
Thursday				
Friday				
Saturday				
Sunday				

Weekly Activity Schedule

	Morning	Midday	Afternoon	Evening
Monday				
Tuesday				
Wednesday				
Thursday				
Friday				
Saturday				
Sunday				

Problem-Solving Worksheet

What is the problem:

___

Why does this problem bother me (what are the specific features that bother me)?

___
___
___

Is this a realistic problem (e.g., what do I really think is going to happen, and what part of this problem do I think is just worry)?

___

How can I rewrite the problem clearly, so that it helps me think about a solution? Write in a clear restatement of the problem:

___
___

Now that I have the problem clearly in mind, what are potential solutions to this problem? To generate solutions, I want to think about as many possible solutions as possible (without thinking why they are good or bad, and without choosing an option at this point). What advice might a good friend give? If a friend had this problem, what advice would I give?

Potential options:

___
___
___
___
___
___

Now rate each potential option. For each option rate the good and bad aspects of the proposed solution. Do not select an option until each is rated.

Good things about each solution   Bad things about each solution

1.
2.
3.
4.
5.
6.

Given this evaluation, which solution seems best?

___

Do you want to apply this solution, or is more time or more information needed to solve this problem?

___

Problem-Solving Worksheet

What is the problem:
_____

Why does this problem bother me (what are the specific features that bother me)?
_____
_____
_____

Is this a realistic problem (e.g., what do I really think is going to happen, and what part of this problem do I think is just worry)?
_____

How can I rewrite the problem clearly, so that it helps me think about a solution? Write in a clear restatement of the problem:
_____
_____

Now that I have the problem clearly in mind, what are potential solutions to this problem? To generate solutions, I want to think about as many possible solutions as possible (without thinking why they are good or bad, and without choosing an option at this point). What advice might a good friend give? If a friend had this problem, what advice would I give?

Potential options:
_____
_____
_____
_____
_____
_____

Now rate each potential option. For each option rate the good and bad aspects of the proposed solution. Do not select an option until each is rated.

Good things about each solution   Bad things about each solution

1.
2.
3.
4.
5.
6.

Given this evaluation, which solution seems best?
_____

Do you want to apply this solution, or is more time or more information needed to solve this problem?
_____

Problem-Solving Worksheet

What is the problem: _____

Why does this problem bother me (what are the specific features that bother me)?
_____
_____
_____

Is this a realistic problem (e.g., what do I really think is going to happen, and what part of this problem do I think is just worry)?
_____

How can I rewrite the problem clearly, so that it helps me think about a solution? Write in a clear restatement of the problem:
_____

Now that I have the problem clearly in mind, what are potential solutions to this problem? To generate solutions, I want to think about as many possible solutions as possible (without thinking why they are good or bad, and without choosing an option at this point). What advice might a good friend give? If a friend had this problem, what advice would I give?

Potential options:
_____
_____
_____
_____
_____
_____

Now rate each potential option. For each option rate the good and bad aspects of the proposed solution. Do not select an option until each is rated.

Good things about each solution   Bad things about each solution

1.
2.
3.
4.
5.
6.

Given this evaluation, which solution seems best?
_____

Do you want to apply this solution, or is more time or more information needed to solve this problem?
_____

Problem-Solving Worksheet

What is the problem:
_____

Why does this problem bother me (what are the specific features that bother me)?
_____
_____

Is this a realistic problem (e.g., what do I really think is going to happen, and what part of this problem do I think is just worry)?
_____

How can I rewrite the problem clearly, so that it helps me think about a solution? Write in a clear restatement of the problem:
_____

Now that I have the problem clearly in mind, what are potential solutions to this problem? To generate solutions, I want to think about as many possible solutions as possible (without thinking why they are good or bad, and without choosing an option at this point). What advice might a good friend give? If a friend had this problem, what advice would I give?

Potential options:
_____
_____
_____
_____
_____

Now rate each potential option. For each option rate the good and bad aspects of the proposed solution. Do not select an option until each is rated.

Good things about each solution   Bad things about each solution

1.
2.
3.
4.
5.
6.

Given this evaluation, which solution seems best?
_____

Do you want to apply this solution, or is more time or more information needed to solve this problem?
_____

Problem-Solving Worksheet

What is the problem:

___

Why does this problem bother me (what are the specific features that bother me)?

___
___
___

Is this a realistic problem (e.g., what do I really think is going to happen, and what part of this problem do I think is just worry)?

___

How can I rewrite the problem clearly, so that it helps me think about a solution? Write in a clear restatement of the problem:

___
___

Now that I have the problem clearly in mind, what are potential solutions to this problem? To generate solutions, I want to think about as many possible solutions as possible (without thinking why they are good or bad, and without choosing an option at this point). What advice might a good friend give? If a friend had this problem, what advice would I give?

Potential options:

___
___
___
___
___
___

Now rate each potential option. For each option rate the good and bad aspects of the proposed solution. Do not select an option until each is rated.

Good things about each solution   Bad things about each solution

1.
2.
3.
4.
5.
6.

Given this evaluation, which solution seems best?

___

Do you want to apply this solution, or is more time or more information needed to solve this problem?

___

CPSIA information can be obtained at www.ICGtesting.com
Printed in the USA
BVOW050834210313

316098BV00005B/9/P